I KNEW HER
The Domestic Violence Conversation Guide

Angle B. Fant

Published 2/14/2017

Printed in the United States of America
ISBN: 978-1-365-75302-2

For imagery details please see https://pixabay.com/en/service/terms/

Acknowledgement

The process of leaving an abuser can be brutal in every way imaginable. It's a dark place to be and during the time when you are adjusting to having made such a major decision, it's a tremendous blessing to have listeners who support and don't judge you. My deepest gratitude to my pastors (Michael Smith Sr. and Timothy Bibb), my mother(Angela Powell),my father(John Powell) my mentor(Tommy Priest), and my editor(Olivia Bethea).

This book is dedicated to my children and my father.

I KNEW HER

Introduction

It was 8 o'clock in the morning. "Are you sure you're making the right decision?" she asked herself.

She got the call and she thought, "He will admit he messed up. Perhaps he will say, sorry and let's work this out." As if he had ever said that before.

He wanted to take her for lunch, so she rode with him. He asked, "You're not going to ask for more money, are you?" "No," she said. They ate lunch and then rode to court. They actually sat together, which felt quite weird.

They arrived at court. The judge was someone they knew. She was completely nervous because the last time she was in the same court room with him was 12 years ago. This was when she was pressured to press charges against him by her aunt. Her aunt was right to tell her to press charges, given that he'd beaten her for 3 hours while she was pregnant.

But, this book isn't about that.

It seemed like the longest wait ever and then, finally, it was time to proceed. The divorce was finalized. She quietly asked for nothing more than her life back. She was free now because she had drawn a line. They rode back to his apartment, where her car was parked.

He asked, "Let's have sex and celebrate?" Horrified, she replied, "Absolutely not!"

There was silence as she walked to her car. She didn't realize this would hurt like hell. She told herself: "Be happy, this is a happy moment."

She felt free, but only for the moment. Minutes, hours, days, weeks, and months passed and she realized that she was still in captivity.

People were saying things like, "Get over it", "She should have stayed", "She is aging, and she used to be beautiful." One comment in particular that she couldn't seem to get out of her head was, "Why did you let him drag you down like that?" In loneliness and solitude, she wrestled with figuring out who she really was.

I realize now, that everyone had something to say.

I now say, *I knew her.* She was me. This book is what I now know as both a survivor of abuse and a resourceful bystander.

Let's become equipped to be a great resource by learning a few Do's and Don'ts as it pertains to having conversations with domestic violence victims who may be in your life or who may come across your path.

The Domestic Violence Conversation Guide

What do you say?

I separated from my husband after a long time of prayer, fasting, and talking to God. I was struggling with depression, because I knew he would not support our family during the time of our separation. My depression was so severe that my doctor took me out of work for two weeks, although he recommended 6 weeks. One of my biggest concerns was that my employer would terminate me. They had already terminated a lot of people to save the company money and a few of them were folks that I had trained.

I reached out to my resource manager to let him know I was struggling with some pretty severe personal challenges. I asked to be demoted into a position of less responsibility but my manager liked my leadership skills and therefore declined my request. Additionally, I was the only one left in my department who knew how to handle key aspects of the business.

I handled a variety of department financial transactions. I had developed ideas to improve customer service, and I trained many of the new lower paid workers so I was a valuable team member.

As things got progressively worse at home, I finally decided to demand that my ex-husband leave. After doing so, I took the two weeks off that my doctor's note allowed. I spent most of that two weeks in bed doing only the most essential things like taking my children to school, picking them up, and fixing them dinner. I was in such a state of despair that I don't even remember even helping with their homework.

At the end of the two weeks my dad, John called me and said he was coming to get me. When I asked where we were going, he said we were going walking. Since I love to walk, I said okay. We ended up walking 8 miles that day. As we walked, my dad reminded me that I am one of the strongest women he knows. He encouraged me that I was strong enough to see this through. His encouragement was welcomed and reminded me that I'd come too far to turn back now.

When the time came for me to return to work, God revealed to me that I would be fired, and sure enough, I was let go the same day I returned before I even clocked in.

I sought help and even asked if I could possibly work in the customer call center in a different department but they declined my request.

So just when I most needed a job with great pay and benefits, one of the main things that any single mother needs----I was terminated.

As devastating as this was for me, what stands out most about this time is the words of encouragement from my father, reminding me that I could do it.

Never underestimate the power of words---sometimes even the simplest encouragement, makes a huge difference.

WHEN THAT HAPPENS, HOW DOES IT MAKE YOU FEEL?

do you feel safe?

Do you know you're loved by friends and family?

Do you know you are worth so much more?

Do you have a plan for getting out?

How can I help you?

You can always talk to me and I mean it.

No pressure, call me anytime.

1-800-799-SAFE (7233) National Domestic Violence Hotline

There are programs available to help you.

It's okay to cry.

You deserve better.

I am proud of you for reaching out to me.

Find someone you can trust.

I think you should seek professional help soon.

What makes you think this is okay?

You can do anything you put your mind too.

Silence hurts more, so feel free to talk.

Do you need help?

How can I assist you?

Have you sought professional assistance?

Do you have somewhere to go?

How do you feel?

Are you hurt?

Do we need to take you to the hospital?

Do you want to contact the police?

Asking questions helps you know how to help. The fact that you see them up close is beneficial. Observe their body language. Pay attention to their reactions as well as their words. Listening is your best tool.

More Questions to Ask

Do you want to press charges?
How were you assaulted?
Do you live with this person?
Do you have children with this person?
Why are you afraid of them?
What makes you stay?
Do you think you deserve this?
How is life for you right now?
Are you financially stable?
What's going on?
How are you?
Where do you live?
Where do you live right now?
Do your children live with you?
Have you and/or your children been hurt in anyway?
Do you want to leave?
What are you thinking?

How are you feeling?

One day you will find true love.

Love doesn't hurt this way, right? Where were you hit?

What are you going to do about it?

Will you please consider a support group or counselling?

Healing Terminology

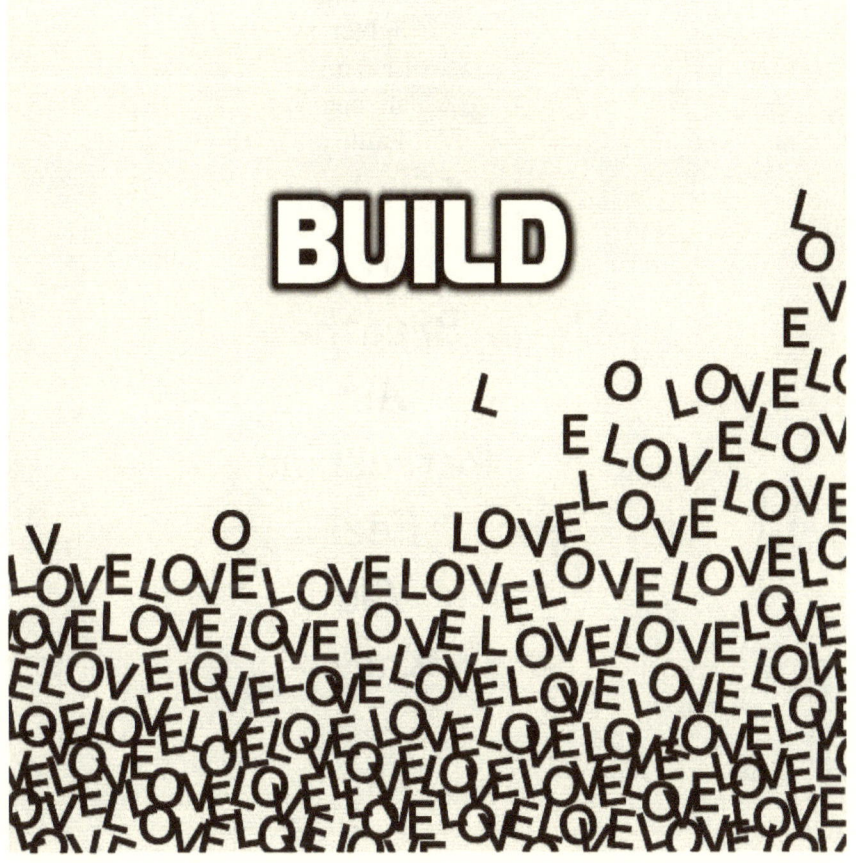

Worthy
Like
Hope
Self
Defense
Protection
Fighter
Listen
Patience
Faith

Survivor

Live

Breathe

Air

Refreshing

Feel

You

Know

Change
Empowerment
Conquer
Courage
Prayer
Pray
Mediate
Smart
Strong
Strength
Powerful
Complete
Wisdom
Stand
Alive
Loyal
Honest
Happiness
Dreams
Forgive
Learn
Lead
Bless
Wonderful
Thankful

Remember
Mirror
Purpose
Family
Trust
Home
Hope
I
Me
Self
Higher
Work
Peace
God
Friends
Resourceful
Blossom
New
Memory
Beauty
Worthy
True
Shared
Light

AMAZING
CONFIDENT
YOU
GIVING
ACCEPT
OPENNESS
PROSPER
SPECIAL
SOUL
SPIRIT
HEART
REVIVE
IMPORTANT
PROUD
DETERMINATION
JOY
HARVEST
BRAVE
KNOWLEDGE
EFFICIENT

If you are the friend or loved one of a victim, just remember that listening and speaking words of encouragement are both tremendously powerful. You need to be aware that many victims go back as many as 7 times before making the final decision to leave. I stayed with my abuser for 16 years before I finally reached the breaking point mentally, physically, spiritually, sexually, and emotionally.

The weight of the situation was so oppressive that it felt like I had a fatal disease and was dying inside. It seemed that the energy surrounding me and even the air I breathed was toxic.

I didn't fully realize just how bad the situation was until after the divorce. I now see that once it's over, both parties receive freedom and a new beginning. If you are reading this and are an abuser, I encourage you to leave the person you are abusing. You are a victim of your anger. Please seek professional help.

Don't Say?

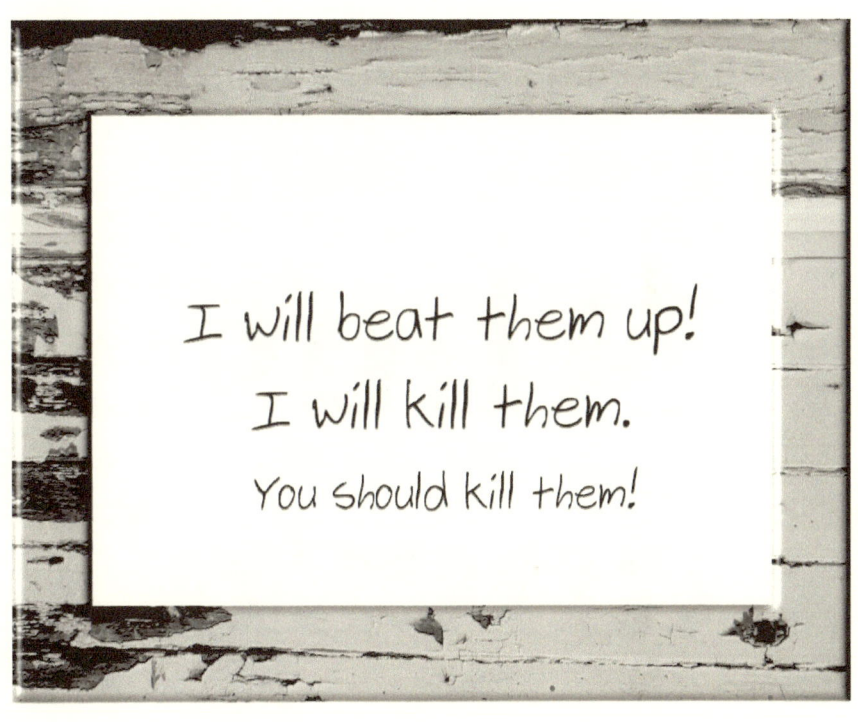

I will beat them up!
I will kill them.
You should kill them!

Abuse doesn't matter.

They pay the bills.

Give them time, they will cool off.

They are just upset. Give them time, they will change.

They are just young and don't know better.

They just don't know how to love and you all are young.
They are just stuck in their ways.

Just pray for them.

They will leave on their own.

It's the only family you have.

They are all you've got.

It's your first love.

- It only happened one time.

- You can't leave.

- But they know God.

- You must submit to the abuser, if you took vows.

- You can't break your vows.

- You can only leave, if they cheat on you.

- Have patience for his and/or her temper.

- Don't leave.

- Don't put them out.
- You can stay with me and the abuser knows where you live.

Well, is sex good? As long as he or she pays the bills, it doesn't matter.

You're not that good looking, you will never find anyone else.

You're getting old, it's hard to find love.

No one will take care of you better.

It just hurts for a little while.

Well, they're going to marry you.

They are going to kill you.

It's not rape, you're married.

You made vows till death do you part.

IT'S HARD BEING ALONE.

You won't make it by yourself.

It's because you talk too much.

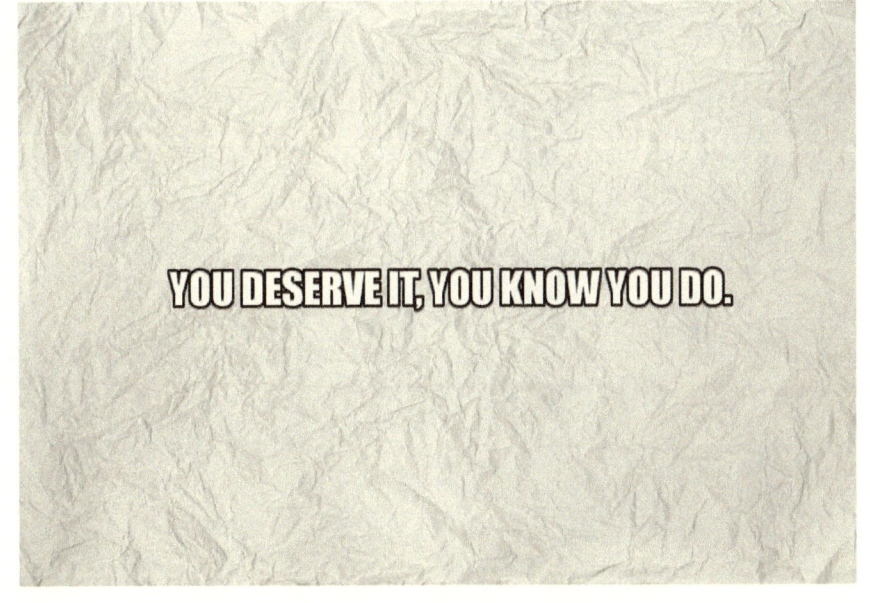

YOU DESERVE IT, YOU KNOW YOU DO.

This is normal for relationships.

Or

WOMEN GO THROUGH THESE THINGS.

YOU JUST HAVE TO ADJUST.

That's how love feels.

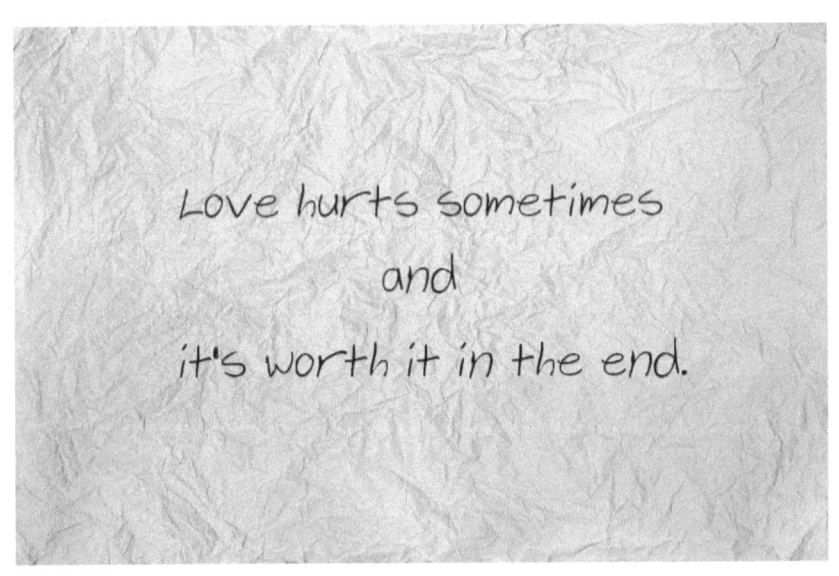

Love hurts sometimes
and
it's worth it in the end.

BE PATIENT

LOVE IS A STRANGE THING.

You must take the bitter with the sweet.

Just put that make up on
and
don't tell anyone.

ACT LIKE IT DOESN'T HURT.

Why Do Victims Stay?

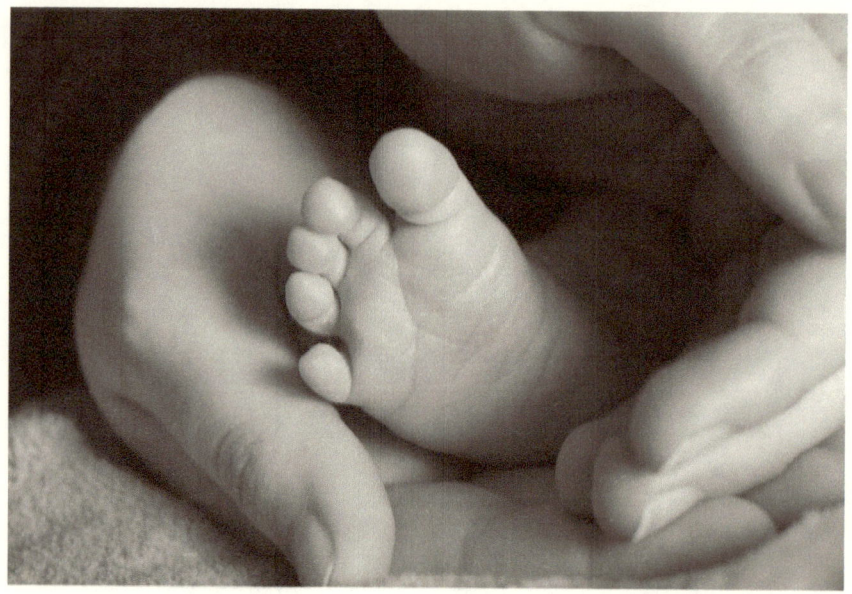

So many people have asked me this question. Why do they stay? At one point, "they" was me!

Being honest, from my perspective, when you're in an abusive situation, it can sometimes be extremely hard to distinguish between good versus bad. Often the mindset of someone who is being abused, but who is in love with their abuser is so muddled, that they can't fully process the abuse. This is why in many cases, they first they blame themselves. Despite the physical pain that they endure at the hands of their abuser they use the flawed reasoning that the good times outweigh the bad. Thinking like this offers little solace. Life with an abuser is life spent walking on eggshells. You never know when the abuser will strike, or when the time bomb is going to detonate.

In fairness, I do remember some really special moments. But, I also remember the unending feeling of not being good enough. I remember being called a whore and am still occasionally called that to this day both by my ex-spouse and the new woman in his life.

I remember not being able to handle money in a way that was acceptable to him. Since I was constantly criticized and lived in fear of messing up, I remember providing receipts for everything I purchased. Even with me going to these extra measures to satisfy him, he wasn't pleased. He often complained that I took too long at the store and suggested that I had really been somewhere else. I lived with the humiliation of being constantly accused.

There are always many negative memories. But among all the painful remembrances there are also a few positive ones like the birth of one's children, or the day one got married. In some cases, the positive memories are about being sexually fulfilled despite the domestic violence. This can be especially true if the person comes from a history of sexual abuse.

Another reason that people stay in abusive relationships is because of the reactions and opinions of bystanders in their lives. Friends, family, church members, co-workers, even children can all be bystanders and have an effect on the outcome of how an abused individual deals with the domestic violence directed against them.

I know it may be hard to believe, but one conversation can change everything. A conversation can result in an abuser finally realizing their abusive behavior is wrong. Conversely, a victim could end up leaving their abuser based on the right conversation at the right time with one of the bystanders in their life who has provided survival kits and information on national support. A victim could end up being set free from a cycle of violence, simply because somehow the bystander was equipped with the right knowledge to have a constructive conversation.

Resourcefulness can be powerful!

National Resources

National connections to serve effectively.

National Domestic Violence Hotline 24/7 Trained
Advocates
http://www.thehotline.org/
1-800-799-7233 | 1-800-787-3224 (TTY)

National Coalition Against Domestic Violence
http://www.ncadv.org/
Phone: 303 839 1852
TTY: 303-839-8459
Fax: 303-831-9251
Email: main office@ncadv.org

National Battered Women's Law Project
http://www.bwjp.org/bwjp_home
275 7th Avenue, Suite 1206
New York, NY 10001
Phone: 212-741-9480
FAX: 212-741-6438

National Resource Center on Domestic Violence
http://nnedv.org/
Phone: 800-537-2238
TTY: 888-Rx-ABUSE; 800- 595 -4889
Fax: 717-545-9456

National Clearinghouse for the Defense of Battered
Women
http://www.ncdbw.org/
125 South 9th Street, Suite 302
Philadelphia, PA 19107
TOLL-FREE: 800-903-0111 ext. 3
Phone: 215-351-0010
FAX: 215-351-0779
Womenspace National Network to End Violence Against
Immigrant Women
http://www.immigrantwomennetwork.org/
Phone: 609-394-0136
24 Hour Mercer County Hotline: 609-394-9000
Fax: 609-396-1093
Email: info@womenspace.org

National Support Groups for Grieving
http://www.griefspeaks.com/id76.html

No Punching Bag
www.nopunchingbag.com
Phone: 706-622-8730
Email: info@nopunchingbag.com

Legal Information and Support
http://www.womenslaw.org/

Domestic Violence Angels

Be prepared for the fact that in the aftermath of leaving, you are likely to miss the one you left. This is not unusual, so accept it as part of the process of moving on. In many cases there are years of memories; holidays, birthdays, laughter, pleasant times when there wasn't a conflict. You may still live or work in close proximity or share a common circle of friends and acquaintances. The fact that you have moved on doesn't mean you won't still be plagued with memories of the life you once shared that is no more.

I encourage you to embrace the belief that it's not your fault. It's not your fault if you were the victim, nor is it your fault if you were a bystander.

Domestic violence has several root causes but is often the result of a combination of untreated mental illness and substance abuse. Hopefully this will change as more attention is called to the problem and public awareness about it is raised. The more the public becomes educated about the subject of domestic violence, the less it will be a shameful unspoken secret with which people feel compelled to suffer in isolation and secrecy.

Every instance of domestic violence that is exposed and overcome diminishes the power of another abuser.

In conclusion, our willingness to have open, compassionate, non-judgmental conversations have the potential to save a life.

About the Author

Angle Fant aka Angel is a multifaceted individual who wears many hats: community advocate, visual artist, visual arts instructor, domestic violence survivor, domestic violence victim's advocate, and mother to name a few.

Angel currently serves as a UNCSA ArtistCorps AmeriCorps Visual Arts Instructor in the Winston-Salem, Forsyth County schools. She studied for three years at the UNC School of the Arts. Angel is a survivor of several years of domestic violence and is the mother of three children with whom she has co-founded, No Punching Bag, an organization focused on raising awareness about domestic violence and prevention while integrating the arts.

Angel and her artistically gifted children design and create wearable art in order to fund outreach and events to educate and assist those impacted by domestic violence. Learn more by visiting the website at: www.nopunchingbag.com